EDUCATION, RACE, and the LAW

By Duchess Harris, JD, PhD

WITH CYNTHIA KENNEDY HENZEL

Essential Library

An Imprint of Abdo Publishing | abdobooks.com

Published by Abdo Publishing, a division of ABDO, PO Box 398166, Minneapolis, Minnesota 55439.
Copyright © 2020 by Abdo Consulting Group, Inc. International copyrights reserved in all countries.
No part of this book may be reproduced in any form without written permission from the publisher.
Essential Library™ is a trademark and logo of Abdo Publishing.

Printed in the United States of America, North Mankato, Minnesota.
082019
012020

Interior Photos: Kamil Krzaczynski/AP Images, 5; Teresa Crawford/AP Images, 6; Rawpixel.com/
Shutterstock Images, 11; Monkey Business Images/iStockphoto, 12, 94, 98; North Wind Picture
Archives, 15; Chelsea Self/Glenwood Springs Post Independent/AP Images, 16; World History
Archive/Alamy, 20; PF-(bygone1)/Alamy, 22; Old Paper Studios/Alamy, 24; Don Ryan/AP Images, 27;
Bettmann/Getty Images, 29; Bill Willcox/The Herald-Sun/AP Images, 30–31; David E. Scherman/
The LIFE Picture Collection/Getty Images, 34; Newsday LLC/Contributor/Newsday/Getty Images,
37; iStockphoto, 38; Othell O. Owensby/Houston Chronicle/AP Images, 40; AP Images, 43, 51, 55,
57; Olivier Douliery/MCT/Newscom, 44; Orlin Wagner/AP Images, 46; Will Counts/The Arkansas
Democrat-Gazette/AP Images, 53; University of Texas at Arlington Special Collection/Fort Worth
Star-Telegram Collection/AP Images, 59; J. Walter Green/AP Images, 60; Rick Bowmer/AP Images,
63; Charles Dharapak/AP Images, 64; Monkey Business Images/Shutterstock Images, 65; Gerald
Herbert/AP Images, 66; Prostock Studio/Shutterstock Images, 71; Jim West/Alamy, 73; Reed Saxon/
AP Images, 77; Chris Maddaloni/CQ Roll Call/AP Images, 81; Michael Jung/Shutterstock Images, 85,
97; J. Scott Applewhite/AP Images, 87; Rich Pedroncelli/AP Images, 91; Dave Collins/AP Images, 92

Editor: Alyssa Krekelberg
Series Designer: Becky Daum

LIBRARY OF CONGRESS CONTROL NUMBER: 2019941946
PUBLISHER'S CATALOGING-IN-PUBLICATION DATA

Names: Harris, Duchess, author. | Henzel, Cynthia Kennedy, author.
Title: Education, race, and the law / by Duchess Harris and Cynthia Kennedy Henzel
Description: Minneapolis, Minnesota : Abdo Publishing, 2020 | Series: Race and American law |
        Includes online resources and index.
Identifiers: ISBN 9781532190254 (lib. bdg.) | ISBN 9781532176104 (ebook)
Subjects: LCSH: Race relations--Juvenile literature. | Discrimination in education--Juvenile literature.
        | Racial bias--Juvenile literature. | Discrimination in higher education--Juvenile literature.
Classification: DDC 305.89--dc23

CONTENTS

CHAPTER ONE

LACKING OPPORTUNITIES

I n 2016, Alejandra Ocampo was a senior at Waukegan High School in Waukegan, Illinois. The school district was having financial issues. Between 2011 and 2016, the district lost millions of dollars in state aid and was forced to make budget cuts. At one school in the district, the band practiced in the hall, and dozens of students shared one computer. The district had to search for funds when emergencies struck. For example, once, the district had to tackle two emergencies at the same time. When a water pipe broke, the district was forced to remove asbestos—a mineral that can lead to dangerous health hazards such as cancer—from the area as well as fix the pipe.

Alejandra remembered going to athletic events at other schools and marveling at their facilities. When students from

Waukegan High School struggled financially in the 2000s.

Alejandra Ocampo went to college to study Spanish and education.

other schools came to Waukegan High School, she would hear them talking about how the school's locker room looked like a dungeon.

A large portion of public school funding comes from local taxes, so there can be a drastic difference in school funding between low- and high-income communities. Many of the students in the Waukegan school district come from low-income families. It's also a minority school district with 80 percent Hispanic students and 15 percent black students.[1]

Twenty miles (32 km) away from Waukegan, students live in a different reality. Adlai Stevenson High School in Lincolnshire, Illinois, has a majority population of white students. The school has an espresso bar, various spaces for theater groups to perform, two gymnasiums, and even an Olympic-sized swimming pool.

Matthew Cabrera, who moved in second grade into the school district from the south side of Chicago, Illinois, knows he's lucky to have the opportunity to walk the manicured lawns and wide carpeted hallways of Adlai Stevenson High School. He also is able to take advanced placement courses and play in the school orchestra.

The school district where Adlai Stevenson High School is located spends $18,800 per student each year. Around 98 percent of the kids there will attend college, with most of them going to four-year schools. The district where Waukegan is located spends $12,600 per student each year. Seventy percent of Waukegan students graduate within four years and fewer than half go on to either a two- or four-year college.[2]

Alejandra knew she beat the odds by graduating and then planning to attend college. But she would have liked to attend a high school with better facilities and more opportunities for extracurricular activities. "I feel

Does Money Matter?

Economists Rucker Johnson, C. Kirabo Jackson, and Claudia Persico found that more spending in schools had large effects on students in the long term. According to reporter Valerie Strauss, their research showed "that 10 percent increases in spending increase graduation rates for students from low-income homes by 10 percent."[3]

Increasing populations of Asian or Hispanic students in previously white schools may change the percentages of minority enrollment. In 2015, whites no longer made up the majority of national public school populations or children under five. Before 2025, whites will no longer make up the majority of people under age 30. Los Angeles, California, became a minority white city in 1990, and 12 states are predicted to have minority white populations by 2031. States and local communities will have to address these changing demographics when considering desegregation plans for their schools. In a city such as Los Angeles, most of the students are nonwhite. The country needs these future workers and leaders to get a good education.

like funding is more of a motivational gift than an actual physical gift. It's how it makes you feel about yourself," she said.[4]

EQUAL OPPORTUNITIES IN EDUCATION?

For more than 150 years, minorities in the United States have struggled for opportunities in equal education. Laws have changed, government policies have changed, schools have become—at times—less segregated, then reversed to become more segregated. Today's efforts to recognize issues that create unequal educational opportunities are part of a long history of legal education reform.

Good educational outcomes for students depend on resources such as skilled teachers and a quality curriculum. In a 1990s study of 900 Texas schools, Harvard economist Ronald Ferguson found that teachers played a particularly important role.[5] He found that good teachers—measured by their level of college education, experience, and test scores on licensing exams—were the most important factor in student achievement. A study by Eleanor Armour-Thomas found that 90 percent of the difference in reading and math scores at third, sixth, and eighth grade depended on teacher qualifications.[6]

Research shows that opportunities are almost always unequal between majority white schools and majority black or Hispanic schools. One reason is that minority schools have less funding and therefore less curriculum choice and a lack of quality materials. They tend to be twice the size of majority white schools, with most class sizes being 15 percent larger.[7] On average, teachers in minority schools have less training and experience than teachers in majority white schools. In addition, many teachers leave minority schools because of stressful working conditions,

Opportunities Lost

In the 2014 class-action lawsuit *Cruz vs. California*, Jason Magaña at Jefferson High joined with other students in south Los Angeles schools to demand equal educational opportunities—especially equal instruction time. South Los Angeles schools in lower socioeconomic minority districts didn't offer classes that students needed to pursue their goals of graduating or attending college. Jason, who hoped to be an engineer, was enrolled in a graphics class he had already passed twice. Students were often assigned to classes they had already passed, extra homerooms, or early release because there was no option for the courses they needed. In a settlement agreement, the Department of Education agreed to offer support to six schools that had scheduling problems.

including a lack of support from school administration. In short, students who attend schools where the majority of students are white have more opportunity for success.

WHY SEGREGATION MATTERS

The year 1988 was the high point of school desegregation in the United States. That year, nearly one-half of all African American students attended majority white schools.[8] From 1970 to 1990, as schools were becoming more integrated, tests scores between minorities and whites narrowed on every national test. The results were most dramatic for elementary students. As desegregation progressed, the average scores of African American students rose 54 points and the scores of white students stayed the same.[9]

However, minority students aren't the only beneficiaries of school integration. In 2016, one of the oldest policy think tanks in the country, the Century Foundation, published a report that found "the benefits of K–12 school diversity indeed flow in all directions." The authors noted, "Researchers have documented that students' exposure to other students who are different from themselves and the novel ideas and challenges that such exposure brings leads to improved cognitive skills, including critical thinking and problem-solving."[10]

Diverse schools can help students from different backgrounds understand each other.

POVERTY AND EDUCATION

Researchers have noted that poverty is a good predictor of low student achievement and that poverty is linked to race. High-poverty schools have enrollments of primarily black and Hispanic students.

In 2018, the Charlotte-Mecklenburg Schools (CMS) in North Carolina published a report on the relationship between poverty and education. They found that in low-poverty schools, where fewer than 25 percent of students were eligible for free lunch, 95.2 percent of students graduated. In high-poverty schools, where more than one-half of students were eligible for free lunch, only 77.6 percent of students graduated. The report noted that, "If you are born poor in Charlotte, you are likely to stay that way."[11]

In 2016, the Century Foundation reported that the achievement gap between rich and poor students was almost twice as large as the gap between white and black students. As school segregation returns and the gap between the rich and poor increases, the past and present attempts to supply equal educational opportunities for all students may provide a window into desegregation in the United States. To understand present-day segregation, it is important to understand how the schools today came to be.

DISCUSSION STARTERS

- Why do you think qualified teachers are said to be the most important asset for student achievement?

- Is your school a minority or majority white school? What effect do you think that has had on your education?

- Do you think all schools should be integrated? Explain your reasoning.

CHAPTER TWO

LEGAL SEGREGATION

E arly groups of European colonists living in what became the United States believed that education was important. They opened schools in the first years of the colonies to teach their children to read, write, and do math. As early as 1647, Massachusetts passed a law that all towns with 50 or more families must hire a teacher.[1] The schools were public and instruction was based on religious teachings. These schools were the foundation of the US education system.

During the formation of the United States, the Constitution didn't address education. Schools remained under the states' control and were generally run by local school boards. Most of today's schools are funded by a combination of state funding and local property taxes. Schools in wealthy areas where property is

Some old schoolhouses, such as this one in Eagle, Wisconsin, have been restored for visitors.

worth more and taxes are high tend to be better funded, with high-tech facilities and highly skilled teachers. Schools in poor areas—often areas with large minority populations—usually struggle to provide the basics and have problems attracting quality teachers.

In the 1800s, a large number of immigrants came to the United States. Education was one way to integrate children from immigrant families into US culture. Also, black children often didn't have the same educational opportunities as white children—especially since, during the time of slavery, enslaved people were banned from learning how to read. However, in the North, black people had more access to education. They were

Punishment for Teaching

For years, state laws prohibited educating black people. The 1847 Virginia Criminal Code states, "Any white person who shall assemble with slaves, [or] free negroes . . . for the purpose of instructing them to read or write . . . shall be punished by confinement in the jail . . . and by fine."[2] Margaret Douglass, a former slaveholder in Norfolk, Virginia, was "greatly interested in the religious and moral instruction of [black children], and finding that the Sunday school where they were allowed to attend was not sufficient," she started to teach free black children to write and read.[3] Under the Virginia code, Douglass was arrested in 1853. She claimed ignorance of the law, saying that she thought the law only applied to slaves. However, the jury convicted and fined her. The judge in the case dismissed the fine and sentenced Douglass to one month in jail as an example to others who may be tempted to break the law. In defense of herself, Douglass claimed that she wasn't an abolitionist and wasn't trying to overturn Southern laws.

able to learn how to write and read more often than black people in the South. But in 1860, it's estimated that only 5 percent of black people in the United States could read.[4]

W. E. B. Du Bois

W. E. B. Du Bois studied at Harvard. In 1895, he earned his PhD in History, becoming the first African American to earn a PhD from that school. He became a prominent writer and speaker for the rights of both African Americans and women. He fought particularly hard against the idea that African Americans were an inferior race that shouldn't be encouraged to achieve in higher education. In 1903, he published *The Souls of Black Folk*. In this piece of literature, Du Bois looked at the progress and obstacles black people face, as well as the future advancement of the race.

After the Civil War (1861–1865) and the abolishment of slavery, Congress passed three constitutional amendments to give some underprivileged groups more rights. The Thirteenth Amendment in 1865 abolished slavery. The Fourteenth Amendment in 1868 gave all citizens equal rights, and the Fifteenth Amendment in 1870 gave African American men the right to vote. No women of any race were allowed to vote at that time. Although the right to vote and abolishing slavery were vital to providing equal opportunity for many citizens, it was the Fourteenth Amendment, which contained what is called the "equal protection clause," that civil rights proponents used in the legal battle for equal educational opportunities. The equal protection clause prohibited states from passing laws that didn't treat all individuals equally under the law.

Also in 1870, the federal government opened the first residential schools for Native American children. Students were separated from their families to live at schools off the reservations. They were given European names and weren't allowed to speak Native languages. They dressed and wore their hair like white people did and ate the food of white people. Many children faced harsh beatings at these schools and were malnourished. Often, the government was more interested in using the schools as a means of conquering the Native American tribes by erasing Native culture than educating children.

PLESSY V. FERGUSON

Despite the assurances guaranteed in the Constitution, black citizens in the South began to see their rights erode around 1877. State legislatures began to pass what were called Jim Crow laws to segregate the society, which included school segregation. Separating the races affected many aspects of people's lives. For example, in 1887, Florida was the first state to segregate railroad cars, and other states quickly did the same.

In 1892, Homer Plessy, who was of mixed race, bought a railroad ticket in Louisiana. He took a seat in a car reserved for white riders. When the conductor ordered that Plessy sit in the car for black riders, Plessy refused and was arrested. He was convicted of violating the law requiring segregated railway

The *Plessy v. Ferguson* ruling eventually led to inequality between black and white schools. White schools often had benefits such as superior materials and better-paid teachers.

cars. Plessy filed a petition against the judge, John H. Ferguson, for violating the equal protection clause of the Fourteenth Amendment. The case went to the Supreme Court.

In 1896, the Supreme Court made its ruling. It decided that separate but equal facilities were constitutional on intrastate railroads. In the court opinion, it was stated that the Fourteenth Amendment applied only to political rights, such as voting, and not to social rights, such as eating in a restaurant, riding a bus, or going to school. Separate but equal became the law of the land and applied to everything in public life, including transportation, lodging, recreational facilities, prisons, the military, churches, and schools. The result of the ruling was a segregated society where the races mixed as little as possible. In education, many people believed that children of formerly enslaved people would be better off in their own schools in their own communities rather than attending white schools.

Under the *Plessy v. Ferguson* ruling, states with public education programs had to tailor education for everyone, although schools could be desegregated or segregated. However, in states that chose segregation, the facilities were seldom equal. In 1899, in *Cumming v. Board of Education of Richmond County*, the Supreme Court upheld the board of education's decision to close a Georgia high school attended by 60 black students. Richmond County wanted to use the space instead for 200 black elementary students.[5] The court's decision was based on Georgia's state constitution. The constitution required that state taxes support elementary education but didn't apply the same rule to high schools. Black students, the court decided, had the option of attending private high schools if they wanted to stay in school.

NAACP

Many people realized that the policy of separate but equal didn't provide equal opportunities to people of color. In 1909, both white and black activists began to challenge the law. They joined to form an organization that became the National Association for the Advancement of Colored People (NAACP). A 1910 document

listed one of the necessary steps to obtain their goal was "that there be equal educational opportunities for all and in all the States, and that public school expenditure be the same for Negro and white child[ren]."[6]

One of the NAACP's early victories was *Buchanan v. Warley*, argued by NAACP president and constitutional lawyer Moorfield Storey. In 1917, the Supreme Court struck down a Louisville, Kentucky, law that discriminated against blacks purchasing or renting property in white neighborhoods. This case had far-reaching consequences for education because by segregating neighborhoods, the law also segregated neighborhood public schools that pulled children from those neighborhoods. This issue has had ramifications even today, as segregation is often a result of geography rather than law.

In 1922, Charles Garland, a student at Harvard University in Massachusetts, donated $800,000 he inherited from his father to found an organization dedicated to social reform. The group, the Garland Foundation, gave $100,000 to the NAACP,

Founding the NAACP

The NAACP was founded in 1909 by people of different races and genders who were concerned about racial violence such as lynchings and race riots. In 1908, whites had rioted in Springfield, Illinois, when police refused to hand over black men accused of crimes. The result was six deaths and hundreds of thousands of dollars of destroyed property. The NAACP grew over the years, and by 1919 the organization had 300 separate branches and about 90,000 members.[7]

In the 1920s, Harvard University discriminated against applicants. In particular, it tried to limit how many Jewish students attended the school.

which used the money in part to hire attorney Nathan Margold to study inequality.[8] Margold focused his research on inequality in public schools. Based on his findings, Margold recommended that the NAACP pursue cases of unequal funding in public schools leading to inequality, a violation of the Supreme Court's interpretation of the Fourteenth Amendment in *Plessy v. Ferguson*.

Charles H. Houston

Charles H. Houston designed the legal strategy that led to the overturn of *Plessy v. Ferguson*. Houston served in World War I (1914–1918). He became an advocate for civil rights in response to the racism he found in the army. He earned a PhD from Harvard Law School in 1923. He then became a professor and eventually the dean at Howard University Law School, where many black students studied to be lawyers. Houston was a mentor to many black leaders who fought to overturn the separate but equal doctrine and for civil rights—including future Supreme Court justice Thurgood Marshall.

Instead, Charles H. Houston, the legal strategist for the NAACP, decided to take another route. He wanted the NAACP to focus its attention on discrimination cases in higher education. He believed that white Southerners would view integrating higher education as less threating compared with integrating public schools. Then, the higher education cases could be used to lay the groundwork for fighting discrimination in all schools.

DISCUSSION STARTERS

- Do you think it is possible to have equal but separate schools for different races? Why or why not?

- Why do you think that it was unlawful to educate enslaved people before the Civil War?

- Why are organizations such as the NAACP important?

NATIVE AMERICAN STUDENTS AND SCHOOLS TODAY

Native American students who attend schools on or near reservations tend to face discrimination. For example, in 2013 the Wiyot Tribe in California filed a complaint over discrimination at a nearby school district. The US Department of Education launched an investigation that lasted almost four years. It was discovered that a principal in the district said that Native students were "a pack of wolves."[9] The principal was also found to have used physical violence against Native students. As a result of the investigation, the school district said it would change its practices.

In addition, many schools with a high Native student population don't have access to a quality education. In 2017, parents filed a lawsuit against the federal government on behalf of Havasupai Elementary School. This Arizona school is located in the Grand Canyon within a community where members of the Havasupai Tribe live. Reporter Alden Woods explained the condition of the school that led to the lawsuit: "Havasupai Elementary . . . has long let down Native American students. The school teaches only English and math. . . . There is no school library. There are no extracurricular activities. Students with disabilities are often just sent home. . . . There's been a rotation of principals and a regular teacher shortage that has caused the school to close for weeks at a time."[10] The tribe asked the government for help multiple times, but their pleas went unanswered. In 2018, a federal court said the US government needed to address the needs of students in schools run by the Bureau of Indian Education, which includes Havasupai Elementary.

In part because of these factors, Native students face struggles in their education. According to Susan Brenna, the editor-in-chief for *One Day* magazine, when it comes to Native students, "no group of students in America fails to graduate or achieve proficiency at such disproportionate rates."[11] The *New York Times* and ProPublica—a nonprofit news organization—looked at federal data and found that Native students struggle more than other demographic groups. For example, on national exams Native students have lower test scores than other groups. In addition, only around 72 percent of these students reach graduation.[12] That's the lowest graduation rate of any group.

It was once illegal to teach Native languages in schools, but today many Native nations are bringing back their languages and teaching children to speak them.

CHAPTER THREE

BREAKTHROUGHS IN HIGHER EDUCATION

I n the first half of the 1900s, most universities were segregated. Every state offered higher education to white students, but the number of black colleges was limited. Houston's strategy for desegregating schools was to begin with students denied opportunities in higher education. States wouldn't be able to fund equal opportunities for black students in separate colleges, especially at the graduate level, due to the high cost of professors and facilities such as laboratories.

The first case that attempted to desegregate higher education was *Hocutt v. Wilson* in 1933. The case began when Thomas R. Hocutt, a 24-year-old student at the North Carolina College for Negroes, applied to the all-white North Carolina School of Pharmacy. He was denied admission due to his race.

Charles H. Houston participated in many Supreme Court civil rights cases.

The name of the North Carolina College for Negroes changed many times. In 1969, it was renamed North Carolina Central University.

The case was dismissed when Hocutt couldn't prove that he was eligible for graduate school because the president of the North Carolina College for Negroes, James E. Shepard, wouldn't release Hocutt's grades. Shepard didn't want the all-white school opened to blacks because he hoped to get state money to enlarge his own school by adding a graduate program for blacks.

Despite the lack of success in the *Hocutt* case, the NAACP was inspired by it and continued efforts to integrate state graduate and professional schools. In 1935, Donald Gaines Murray, a graduate of Amherst University, was denied entry into law school at the University of Maryland. When he sued for admission, Houston and future Supreme Court justice Thurgood Marshall represented him.

Marshall had himself been denied entry into the law school based on his race. He attended the all-black Howard Law University in Washington, DC, for his law degree. Marshall argued that attending an out-of-state law school wasn't equal because state laws differed. A lawyer educated in one state wouldn't know state laws as well as a lawyer educated in the state where he or she practiced.

Thurgood Marshall

Thurgood Marshall (1908–1993) founded the NAACP Legal Defense and Educational Fund, the legal arm of the NAACP, in 1940. He was also the attorney who guided the defense in the *Brown v. Board of Education* case that overturned the separate but equal doctrine in US law. A champion of civil rights, Marshall argued 32 cases before the US Supreme Court.[1] He was also the first black US Supreme Court justice, serving from 1967 to 1991.

The Maryland Supreme Court ruled for the plaintiff in the case, *Murray v. Pearson*. The court stated that Murray couldn't be denied entry based on race because there was no equal facility for him to attend. Murray became the first black law graduate from the University of Maryland since 1890. The decision only affected the state of Maryland, as it was decided by the Maryland Supreme Court rather than the US Supreme Court. Still, Marshall's success in the case launched his career as one of the premier civil rights lawyers in the country.

NOT ALL SUCCESS

In 1935, the NAACP was involved in another higher education case, *Gaines v. Canada*. Lloyd Gaines had graduated with honors from Lincoln University, an all-black college in Missouri. He applied to the law school at the University of Missouri at Columbia. He was denied admission. The Missouri state constitution denied admission to blacks at all University of Missouri colleges. However, the state would pay tuition for him to attend an out-of-state college to meet the demands for equal opportunity under the Fourteenth Amendment.

Gaines sued the university and the state, citing that sending him out of state did not provide equal education to being admitted to the state law school. The state judge ruled that the state would pay tuition for him to attend an out-of-state college, or Gaines could apply to Lincoln University, the black college he had attended, and that school would provide law instruction. Since this would in no way provide equal opportunity to an established law university, the case went to the US Supreme Court.

The Supreme Court determined that the state had to admit Gaines to the University of Missouri law school or build and staff a separate law school providing the same education he would receive from the University of Missouri. Despite the cost of building a separate facility, the state didn't budge on its policy and instead opened the Lincoln University School of Law to educate black students. The facility remained open for the next 16 years until *Plessy v. Ferguson* was overturned.

THE END OF WORLD WAR II

World War II (1939–1945) showed the plight of black citizens in the United States. Many black men and women served in the US

The Mystery of Lloyd Gaines

Although Lloyd Gaines's demand for equal education brought about the Lincoln University School of Law, he never attended the college. Shortly after winning his case in the Supreme Court, Gaines disappeared before he could talk about whether he felt the hastily assembled school could provide an education equal to the University of Missouri Law School. He was last seen in Chicago after telling friends he was going out to buy stamps. His fate is unknown. Some people believe he was murdered, kidnapped and lynched, or bribed to disappear. Others theorized that he simply ran away due to the pressures he faced. In 1995, the University of Missouri offered a scholarship in honor of Gaines. In 2006, the University of Missouri awarded him a law degree posthumously. In addition, the Missouri Supreme Court awarded him an honorary law license.

Black soldiers from World War II were looked down upon by some white people after coming home to the United States.

military during the war. Yet when they returned home, they were once again treated as second-class citizens. Many black veterans couldn't take advantage of the Veteran's Administration (VA) benefits under the GI Bill. The GI Bill was meant to help veterans of the war. One lost benefit included home loans with low interest rates because banks wouldn't loan black veterans money for houses.

Another benefit involved help with paying for college tuition. However, black veterans of World War II weren't able to take advantage of this opportunity because they couldn't attend many segregated universities. Those they could attend were overcrowded and had fewer resources. By 1946, only 20 percent of the 100,000 black applicants for VA educational benefits were attending colleges.[2] Although black veterans weren't able to take advantage of their benefits as much as white veterans, some who did attend universities became leaders of future civil rights struggles.

BUYING PROPERTY

One important case helped set a legal precedent on segregated communities, which often led then—and still leads today— to segregation of schools. In 1917, the Supreme Court had determined in *Buchanan v. Warley* that zoning restrictions that prohibited selling property to blacks were unconstitutional. The court ruled that these laws violated the due protection clause of the Fourteenth Amendment because they infringed on the rights of property owners to sell to whomever they wanted. However, white neighborhoods tried to bypass this decision by making private covenants, or agreements, within a community that stated that no one in the community would sell or rent to an African American.

In 1948, the Supreme Court ruled on a case, *Shelley v. Kraemer*, in which a white man filed a lawsuit against the Shelleys, a black couple, to force them to give up a house they had bought in a white neighborhood. The neighborhood had a covenant that didn't allow selling houses to blacks. The court determined that covenants between private citizens restricting selling or renting to blacks in a neighborhood weren't illegal. However, a state couldn't enforce a covenant because states were under the jurisdiction of the Fourteenth Amendment. Therefore, the state couldn't force the Shelleys to sell their property. This meant that residents of white neighborhoods couldn't keep black students out of neighborhood schools by refusing to sell property to black families.

BUILDING A BODY OF LAW

The NAACP continued trying cases that would build a body of law to serve as a precedent for desegregating schools. One of their targets was Texas, a wealthy oil state. Texas had already run out of funding to send black students out of state for graduate school. If the NAACP could show that even Texas couldn't afford to build a separate but equal law school, it would indicate to other states that separate but equal graduate schools were too expensive.

Covenant Recusals

Covenants to keep black people from living in white neighborhoods were common. In 1948, when the US Supreme Court heard the case of *Shelley v. Kraemer*, three of the nine Supreme Court justices had to disqualify themselves. They lived in neighborhoods that had private covenants between property owners forbidding sale of property to African Americans.

In the 2000s, Gregory L. Fenves, the president of the University of Texas at Austin, acknowledged the school's past of segregation. He said that the school today strives to be a champion of diversity.

In 1946, the NAACP asked for volunteers to be the plaintiff in a case to integrate the University of Texas. Heman Marion Sweatt had the prerequisite education and a desire to get a law degree, so he volunteered and applied to the University of Texas. He was denied entry based on his race. With the help of the NAACP, he filed a lawsuit. A Texas court determined that the state must provide an equal facility or admit Sweatt. One year later, the university opened the School of Law of the State University for Negroes. When Sweatt found that the new campus had only one or two professors and no other students, he went back to court. In 1950, the US Supreme Court decided in *Sweatt v. Painter* that the law school for African Americans was inferior and ordered that Sweatt be allowed into the University of Texas Law School.

Around the same time, George W. McLaurin filed a suit with the federal court in Oklahoma. His case was against the University of Oklahoma on the grounds that he was denied entry for an advanced degree in education based on his race. The court ruled that McLaurin couldn't be denied admission, but the university decided to segregate him on campus. He was allowed to attend class but had his desk placed in an adjacent space. He could hear the teacher's instruction but, at first, he wasn't visible to the white students in the class. He also had to sit at a separate table in the library and cafeteria. McLaurin filed an appeal with the US Supreme Court. Before the ruling, the university decided to allow McLaurin to sit with the students in the classroom— though he was placed in his own row—and gave him a spot in the library and cafeteria.

In the case *McLaurin v. Oklahoma State Regents*, the court ruled that McLaurin's separation kept him from exchanging views with other students and made it more difficult to study and to learn his profession, thus depriving him of equal opportunity.

The *Sweatt* and *McLaurin* cases were important in
establishing that equal facilities didn't mean just buildings. In
both cases, the US Supreme Court decreed that the quality of
the faculty, the reputation of the college, and the network of
alumni available to white students at white universities weren't
equal to what was available at the makeshift universities
that states attempted to set up for black students. The idea
that these intangible qualities of a good university or school
couldn't be recreated would be important in arguing the most
important case in education in the United States: *Brown v. Board
of Education*.

DISCUSSION STARTERS

- How do you think integrating schools dedicated to higher
  education helped integrate K–12 schools?

- Why do you think universities resisted integration?

- Do you think it's fair that white neighborhoods tried to
  stop minorities from moving in? Explain your answer.

CHAPTER FOUR

BROWN V. BOARD OF EDUCATION

I n 1945, Sylvia Mendez, who had Mexican heritage, was going into third grade. She and her siblings were denied entrance into a neighborhood school in Westminster, California. They were told that they must attend a school set aside for children of Mexican ancestry in Orange County.

Sylvia's father, Gonzalo Mendez, and his lawyer, David Marcus, filed suit against the district on behalf of Mendez's kids and 5,000 other children of Latin descent in the county.[1] The suit was known as *Mendez v. Westminster*.

Marcus knew he couldn't win a segregation suit. That's because the doctrine of separate but equal—enshrined by *Plessy v. Ferguson*—was the law of the land. He therefore tried a different approach using arguments from social science.

Linda Brown was one of the plaintiffs in *Brown v. Board of Education* when she was a young girl.

In 2011, Sylvia Mendez received a Presidential Medal of Freedom.

Marcus argued that segregation produced feelings of inferiority in Mexican American students. These feelings made the students less productive.

US District Court judge Paul McCormick agreed with the plaintiff. He ordered the county to cease segregation in its schools. McCormick also noted that public schools between blacks and whites were not equal. Upon appeal, the US Court of Appeals upheld the determination. Governor Earl Warren signed a bill two months later that ended segregation in California. It was the first state to officially end segregation, but the issue remained open in other states because the case had not gone to the US Supreme Court.

The NAACP entered the case during the appeal process as a friend of the court—a person or organization with strong views or an interest in a case without being a direct participant. Thurgood Marshall wrote the brief outlining the NAACP's arguments. He later used some of Marcus's arguments when he went before the US Supreme Court to try to end school segregation in *Brown v. Board of Education*.

THE *BROWN* CASE

Meanwhile, the NAACP continued to put its emphasis on integrating education. Having successfully integrated many graduate schools, the NAACP had now turned to K–12 public schools. It filed many state lawsuits that failed at the US District Court level due to *Plessy v. Ferguson*. The US Supreme Court case *Brown v. Board of Education* actually resolved various cases. The lawsuits came from Washington, DC, and four states—South Carolina, Virginia, Kansas, and Delaware. Delaware had two cases that were so similar that they were combined into one case. The Kansas case involved Linda Brown, who was rejected from

Lawyer in *Brown*

Constance Baker Motley, born in 1921 to immigrant parents from the West Indies, graduated from Columbia Law School in 1946. She then played an important role in preparing for the *Brown v. Board of Education* case as a lawyer at the NAACP Legal Defense Fund. In 1961, Motley argued her first case before the Supreme Court. In 1964, she became the first black woman in the New York State Senate, and in 1966, she became the first black federal court judge.

The *Brown v. Board of Education* National Historic Site is in Topeka, Kansas.

a white elementary school. Her last name is on the landmark Supreme Court case.

The court decided to hear the cases together because they all concerned the problem of unequal opportunities for black students under the doctrine of separate but equal. Although the *Brown* case specifically involved K–12 schools, the opinion of the court would have far-reaching consequences for all segregated facilities.

On the morning of December 7, 1953—the first of three days of the *Brown* arguments at the Supreme Court—many people were waiting outside for seats in the courthouse. Arguments were to begin that afternoon. Attorney Spottswood Robinson was first to argue for the plaintiffs, followed by Marshall. Marshall, using the tactic from *Mendez*, argued that segregation brought about low self-esteem among African American children.

THE OPINION

The Supreme Court heard the five cases in *Brown v. Board of Education* one after another for three days. The justices then began deliberations, and the country waited more than five months to hear what it would decide. The decision was unanimous. *Brown v. Board of Education* overturned *Plessy v. Ferguson*.

In the written opinion, Chief Justice Earl Warren, who was previously the governor of California, wrote, "Segregation of white and colored children in public schools has a detrimental effect upon the colored children. The impact is greater when it has the sanction of the law, for the policy of separating the races is usually interpreted as denoting

The Doll Study

Kenneth and Mamie Clark had PhDs in psychology and decided to study the effects of segregation on black children in the 1940s. In the experiment, they gave black children four dolls, which were identical except that two dolls were black and two dolls were white. When asked questions about the dolls, the black children in the study were more likely to say the black doll was "bad" compared to the white doll, which was "nice."[2] In addition, many black children said the white dolls looked more like them than the black dolls. The Clarks concluded that forced segregation made black children feel inferior to whites—a feeling that would likely linger with the black children throughout their lives. Marshall used their testimony in *Brown v. Board of Education*.

the inferiority of the Negro group. . . . We conclude that in the field of public education the doctrine of 'separate but equal' has no place. Separate educational facilities are inherently unequal."[3]

Chief Justices and Brown

In 1952, Chief Justice Fred Vinson knew *Brown* would be a difficult case. Vinson doubted the Supreme Court's authority to force integration on the states. Many people felt that without the chief justice's support, the case was doomed to failure. Vinson died in late 1953 and Earl Warren was chosen by President Dwight D. Eisenhower as chief justice. Warren was the previous governor of California who had signed desegregation into law there. The Warren court heard the final arguments of the case.

RESISTANCE TO BROWN

Over the next decade, some schools began to slowly desegregate. But there was massive resistance from white parents who didn't want their children going to school with black students. Many parents began fleeing urban areas for suburbs where they could have their own white school districts. This white flight to the suburbs changed the makeup of cities across the country. The more affluent white families left the urban areas, which then became poorer and home to more minorities. Urban property values dropped, meaning less money for urban schools, which depended on property taxes for funding. Meanwhile, suburban property values increased.

Some parents who opposed desegregation opted for private schools. Private schools could be selective in their student population because they didn't use public funds. Some of these private schools were religious schools funded by churches.

Resistance in some places was more extreme. In Virginia, many white parents opposed any desegregation. When ordered to desegregate in 1959, Prince Edward County closed its schools. Then, the Prince Edward Foundation opened private schools for white students. Money for the schools came from tuition grants from the state and tax credits from the county. Black children in Prince Edward County, Virginia, had no support for public schools.

DISCUSSION STARTERS

- Why do you think Marshall used the *Mendez* tactic when arguing in the *Brown* case?

- Many white people were resistant to school integration after the *Brown* decision. Why do you think that was? Do you think people have the same feelings today? Explain your answers.

- How do you think the African American community felt after the *Brown* decision?

CASES PRESENTED IN *BROWN V. BOARD OF EDUCATION*

Brown v. Board of Education was a combination of five cases that addressed the same issue: discrimination in education aimed at black students.

Briggs v. Elliott
In 1950, parents brought a suit opposing segregation against the school board in Clarendon County, South Carolina. The US District Court ruled that segregation was legal but ordered the school board to ensure equal facilities for black and white students.

Brown v. Board of Education
In 1950, 13 parents in Topeka, Kansas, took their children to be enrolled in white neighborhood schools. The 20 children were refused admission and sent to black schools in the city.[4]

Bolling v. Sharpe
The John Philip Sousa Junior High School in Washington, DC, refused to admit 11 black students in 1950.[5] In the end, the Supreme Court chose to rule on this case separately from the others because DC wasn't a state.

Davis v. County School Board of Prince Edward County
In 1951, high school student Barbara Johns led a two-week strike to protest the horrible conditions of her black Virginia high school. More than 100 students filed suit to overturn the state segregation law.[6] The US District Court ruled against the students but required the school board to equalize the students' school.

Belton (Bulah) v. Gebhart
Two similar court cases were combined into one Delaware case. Some black parents in Delaware were forced to send their children to a distant run-down high school rather than the neighborhood white high school. In 1951, the parents sued because there was no transportation for black children. The court ordered that the black children be admitted to the white school, but the board of education filed an appeal that eventually took the case to the Supreme Court.

From left to right, George E. C. Hayes, Thurgood Marshall, and James M. Nabrit were lawyers who participated in the *Brown* case.

CHAPTER FIVE

INTEGRATION BEGINS

Many schools ignored the order to desegregate, but the NAACP continued its efforts toward equal opportunity in education. In 1957, nine students recruited by the NAACP, known as the Little Rock Nine, tried to enroll in Central High School in Little Rock, Arkansas. On the first day of school, a mob of whites gathered before the school to prevent the students from entering. Arkansas governor Orval Faubus sent the Arkansas National Guard to stop the students.

Lawyers for the NAACP, including Marshall, got a federal order to prevent the governor from barring the students from the school. Under police escort, the students began school. Civil rights leader Martin Luther King Jr. asked President Dwight D. Eisenhower to step in. The president sent troops to protect the

Members of the Little Rock Nine, such as Elizabeth Eckford, received open hostility when trying to attend school.

students for the rest of the year. Ernest Green of the Little Rock Nine was the first black person to graduate from the school.

Still, Faubus refused to accept desegregation. Before the schools opened in 1958, he closed all Little Rock high schools rather than allowing black students to attend. However, the Supreme Court ruled the next year that the city had to reopen the schools and continue with desegregation.

Central High Today

In 1999, President Bill Clinton awarded the Congressional Gold Medal, the highest honor given to civilians, to the Little Rock Nine, the students who integrated Central High School. Today the high school is a national historic site that is also part of the school district. The historic site contains a civil rights museum administered in part by the National Park Service. In 2007, the US Mint created a commemorative silver dollar to "recognize and pay tribute to the strength, the determination and the courage displayed by African-American high school students in the fall of 1957."[2]

ALL DELIBERATE SPEED

The court knew that integrating schools wasn't an easy task, so it gave states time to develop plans for desegregating their schools. However, as time passed, more school districts began to ignore the new ruling against segregation. In 1964, the Department of Health, Education, and Welfare (HEW) found that only 2.4 percent of African Americans attended majority white schools in the South.[1] After years of little or no action, the courts and the federal government began to lose patience.

In response to the increasing demand for civil rights, including equal-opportunity education, Congress passed the Civil Rights Act of 1964. This act outlawed many of the lingering Jim Crow laws that made it more difficult for blacks to vote, get jobs, and even find housing. It gave the US Justice Department the right to file suit against districts for school segregation. The Civil Rights Act also gave HEW the power to define integration. In 1966, these guidelines stated that 16 to 18 percent of black children in all school districts must attend predominantly white schools.[3]

President Lyndon B. Johnson signed the Civil Rights Act in July 1964.

In 1966, a report funded by the federal government in response to the Civil Rights Act found that the most influential factor in school for student achievement was the student body's racial and socioeconomic mix. The federal government pushed harder to get states to comply with the desegregation law. More federal dollars were flowing to schools after the 1964 Civil Rights Act, which gave the federal government the power to pull money from schools for not following desegregation orders.

When a school still didn't work toward desegregation, courts imposed desegregation plans on the districts. For example, in 1965, an attorney for a group of black children filed a lawsuit against the Jefferson County Board of Education in Alabama to end its segregated school system. In 1971, a federal court imposed a desegregation plan on the district. The plan

Experiencing Segregation

Today, Nicole Hannah-Jones is an investigative reporter. As a child, she was bused into a white school in Waterloo, Iowa. Hannah-Jones felt that she got an opportunity for a good education. However, she felt isolated at a high school that was 70 percent white, pointing out that a desegregated school where blacks are allowed to go isn't the same as an integrated school where everyone is equal. In addition, she notes that people should do more than just give money to poor schools: "There are intangible things that you lose when you're in a segregated entirely poor school. And one of those things is that by being isolated from the language and the culture of those who run your country[,] who will run the businesses that you may want to work for, you can't make up for that isolation by throwing more dollars and getting better textbooks."[4]

Some people were very opposed to desegregation.

included changing the zoning lines of neighborhood schools so schools were less segregated. It also revised plans to build new schools so that new construction wasn't primarily in majority white districts.

BUSING

New Kent County, Virginia, had two schools—one on the west side of the county and one on the east side. George W. Watkins school was a black school and New Kent was a white school. There was no effort to desegregate the schools until the court forced the issue ten years after *Brown*. At that time, the county opted for a freedom of choice plan under which students could choose the school they wanted to attend.

No white students chose to attend Watkins. Although 115 black students enrolled in New Kent, 85 percent of black children still attended Watkins.[5] The court found that members of the white community discouraged black children from attending the white school through intimidation and retaliation. Poverty was also a factor, as poor black students were sometimes embarrassed by their lack of nice clothes and money for fees to pay for special classes.

In 1968, the Supreme Court ruled in *Green v. County School Board of New Kent County* that it wasn't enough for school districts to allow students to attend the school of their choice to achieve desegregation. Instead, districts must actively work toward desegregation.

Affirmative Action

Green v. County School Board of New Kent County is often cited as the beginning of affirmative action. Affirmative action is an active effort to improve the conditions of minorities and women in areas where they historically faced fewer opportunities, such as in jobs or education.

However, in the late 1960s, schools across the country still remained segregated. In the Charlotte-Mecklenburg School District in North Carolina, 14,000 of 24,000 African American students still attended all-black schools.[6] The Supreme Court ruled in the case of *Swann v.*

Charlotte-Mecklenburg Board of Education (1971) that forcing students to ride buses to different schools was a legal way to achieve desegregation. The judge ordered the school district to bus students to different schools to achieve integration.

BUSING BACKLASH

Busing was extremely unpopular. In Boston, Massachusetts, black parents had tried unsuccessfully for a decade to force the Boston School Committee to provide equal schools for black students. In June 1974, a federal court finally ruled that students must be bused to achieve desegregation. An anti-busing group held a protest at city hall which turned violent. When school began, police had to escort black students off the buses at white schools.

Housing within school districts was often segregated. Busing was needed to get students out of their neighborhoods and into certain schools to help desegregation efforts.

White protesters threw things at the buses as black children rode in them. Racial tension increased in the fall throughout Boston and flowed into the schools, resulting in a school fight where a white student was stabbed. Desegregation wasn't any easier in the North than in the South.

Parents also objected to lottery programs where students were assigned schools based on randomly drawn names. Students living near one school could end up assigned to a school that was miles from their home. Siblings might end up in different schools. It made planning for school each year difficult, especially because decisions were often not made until just before school started.

DISCUSSION STARTERS

- Do you think busing was an effective way to achieve desegregation?

- Do you think the courts were right to force schools to integrate rather than waiting to see if it would occur naturally? Explain your answer.

- How do you think it would feel to be bused to a school in which you were the minority, such as a black student bused to a mostly white school or a white student bused to a mostly black school?

CHAPTER SIX

CHOICE

Desegregation by choice rather than by court order created several new ideas for drawing white students to minority districts, including vouchers and magnet schools. Voucher programs are scholarships provided to students to pay tuition at private schools. Some states provide them to help students from low-income families, students who want to leave failing schools, students with disabilities, or students in special circumstances such as those living in foster care. The first modern voucher program began in Milwaukee, Wisconsin, in 1989.

Proponents of vouchers say that the money to attend private schools provides parents with choice and increases competition between schools. Opponents point out that vouchers take

Choice in schooling can help parents meet their child's needs.

President George W. Bush supported tuition vouchers.

money from public schools that must still provide for the vast majority of students.

A 2016 study looked at a voucher program in Louisiana. The program gives state money to students so they can go to private schools. It found that the program had made the public schools that students were leaving more integrated. Reporter Hayley Glatter explained the situation: "Researchers found that as families participated in the program, the student bodies of the public schools they opted out of began to more closely reflect the racial makeup of the school's surrounding community."[1] That's because a large number of the students using vouchers were black and leaving a majority black school. This increased the percentage of white students in the school they left. However, this program also made private schools more segregated since more African American students started going there.

MAGNET SCHOOLS

Magnet schools are schools within a district that offer special programs not available in other district schools. They may be themed magnet schools, such as schools that offer a focus in performing arts; music and art; language immersion; or science, technology, engineering, and math (STEM). The US Department of Education offers federal dollars to magnet schools that are in districts under a court-ordered or approved voluntary desegregation plan.

Magnet schools may be anywhere in a district. They are often established in minority neighborhoods as an incentive for white students to travel to attend the magnet school. Without these

Magnet schools have specialized coursework.

incentives, white students are less likely to request transfers to lower-income or minority schools than black students are to higher-quality white schools.

In 2002, Christine H. Rossell of Boston University studied whether magnet schools were an effective tool for desegregation. The actual success of achieving desegregation depended on how well the district used its magnet schools. Placement of magnet schools was also an important consideration. Placing magnet schools in white neighborhoods increased segregation. In addition, having too many magnet schools in a district reduced the number of white students being

Education Secretary Betsy DeVos, *center*, is a strong supporter of charter schools.

pulled into any one magnet school, thus reducing the number of white students in minority schools.

CHARTER SCHOOLS

Public schools are funded by tax dollars and are run by locally elected school boards. Just like public schools, charter schools are funded by tax dollars. However, charter schools are sometimes run by privately owned and operated businesses, for-profit organizations, or parents and teachers. The first charter school opened in Minnesota in 1992. The idea blossomed, and between 2000 and 2015 the number of charters grew from 2,000 to 6,900.[2]

Supporters of charter schools say the institutions are held to high standards, so they must have good results. If they don't, the schools can be shut down. They also note that the schools give families a choice, especially in communities with failing public school systems. They provide competition between public schools, which motivates schools to get better to draw in students. In addition, some charter school teachers are

Capping Voucher Funds

A 2019 report noted that in Wisconsin, around $192.9 million that would have gone to public schools would instead be distributed between the voucher program and charter schools that year.[3] Legislators suggested capping the number of vouchers and eliminating a tax deduction parents receive for private school tuition. This action could help increase funding for public schools.

allowed to be innovative in their teaching methods, which some people believe can benefit students.

Opponents of charter schools say the institutions are hard to control, because the school board is appointed and not elected by the general public. They also claim that charters take away funds from public school districts and don't offer help to as many students with disabilities as public schools do.

Big Business

Individuals or small groups run some charter schools. Others have become big and successful businesses. The Knowledge Is Power Program (KIPP) runs 224 schools across the United States.[4] By 2020 it planned to enroll 120,000 students.[5] Individuals Dedicated to Excellence and Achievement (IDEA) schools plan to serve 40,000 students by then.[6] The schools have waiting lists and admirable educational results. In some communities, such as Washington, DC, approximately one-half of students attend charter schools. In New Orleans, where charters flourished after Hurricane Katrina destroyed many schools, almost all schools are charters.

Although charter schools can't select students based on race or socioeconomic status, they have much more leeway in student selection. Charters may use screening procedures such as parent interviews, essays, letters of recommendation, or attendance records to make a decision about accepting a student. Parents who have low incomes may not be comfortable with interviews or able to provide letters of recommendation. Charters may also consider whether a student needs to attend a special education program that the charter doesn't provide. Public schools, on the other hand, can't turn students away.

CHARTER SCHOOLS AND SEGREGATION

Although white, black, and Hispanic students usually attend charter schools in equal numbers across the country, the charter schools they attend are often more segregated than the schools they leave. In general, with the exception of a few charter schools that emphasize diversity, charter schools tend to be more racially segregated than public schools in the same geographic area.

With many inner-city schools failing, black students often attend charters as their only option to escape inadequate public schools in their neighborhoods. Studies from the Brookings Institution in 2016 show that even though these charter schools are more segregated, they may provide a better option for student achievement than the failing public urban schools.

DISCUSSION STARTERS

- Which school choice option do you think is most effective to achieve racial integration? Explain your answer.

- Do you think public funds should be spent to support nonpublic schools? Why or why not?

- Do you think school vouchers should be provided to all students to attend the school of their choice, whether public or private?

CHAPTER SEVEN

DISCIPLINE IN SCHOOLS

I t was only one day after his eleventh birthday in 2011 when a sixth-grade boy decided to play a prank. He was with some classmates at his elementary school in Bakersfield, California. They ran behind a female classmate. The boy swatted her on the buttocks, shouting, "Want to see what football players do?"[1] Then he and his friends ran away, laughing.

Later, the boy stood sobbing before school officials with his mother, a Hispanic farm labor manager. The school expelled him for the rest of the year. He was also charged with sexual battery and obscenity—a charge usually reserved for much more serious offenses.

In 2010, Patricia Crawford's daughter, a black high school student in Bakersfield, was expelled for a fight that witnesses

Missing school because of a suspension or expulsion can have a negative effect on a student.

agreed she didn't start. Eventually, Crawford's daughter was cleared of wrongdoing, but she fell behind in school during the time the case was being investigated. The school allowed her to return to school, but it still suspended her from playing volleyball. In addition, her school records claimed that she was a problem student, affecting how teachers and others viewed her.

Bakersfield is located in Kern County in the Central Valley of California. The county's schools were known for decades for their rigorous use of suspension and expulsion for school infractions. In 2013, Kern's rate of suspension was three times that of the California average.[2]

Although the district claimed that schools weren't intentionally racist in their disciplinary practices, data showed that Latino and black students were more often targeted with punishment than white students. In 2006, East Bakersfield High School expelled 26 percent of its black students, according to data the school submitted to the US Department of Education as part of a national survey.[3] In 2013, the Center for Public Integrity and KQED radio reported that Kern students were removed from school for minor reasons and placed in alternative schools. Many dropped out or did independent study, which meant only a half-day of interaction with a teacher each week. Others studied at home. Black and Hispanic students assigned to home study routinely fell behind their peers.

During the 2012–2013 school season, 67 percent of black students who were expelled were forced to leave school for reasons that didn't include injuring someone or possessing drugs or weapons.[4] Among white students, only 42 percent were expelled for similar minor infractions.[5] Willful defiance suspensions, such as talking back or coming to class unprepared, were more likely for Latino or black students than for white students.

A lawsuit was filed in 2014 against the district. One of the complaints in the lawsuit was that the school dean asked Jerry

Students have protested school disciplinary policies that disproportionately hurt minority students.

Reagor, a black high school student, to remove his hat one morning. Near the end of the school day, Jerry returned to get his hat and was told that he had to wait because the dean was in a meeting. When several other students came and picked up belongings, he went to knock on the dean's door so he wouldn't be late for class. The school police were called. He was suspended for five days and transferred to an alternative school.

ALTERNATIVE ARRANGEMENTS

As in many states, California law mandates that students who are expelled from school receive alternative arrangements to continue their education. Kern County has a number of community schools, known in some places as alternative schools, for students who are no longer allowed to attend their regular school. Alternative schools seldom provide the choice of classes or extracurricular activities of a regular school.

In the lawsuit filed against Kern High School District in October 2014, parents said that despite meetings with school officials, little had been done to solve the problems of expelling students and placing them in alternative schools that were detrimental to student learning. This was a particular problem with minority students. The district at that time claimed a student enrollment of 55 percent Latino, 32 percent white, and 8 percent black.[6] However, over a five-year period, 60 percent of those expelled were Latino, 22 percent were white, and 15 percent were black.[7] Because discipline fell

Alternative Schools for Minority Students

In the 1970s, the University of California, Berkeley experimented with two alternative schools, Black House and La Casa de la Raza, that were specifically designed around the shortcomings of white-designed schools for minority students. The theory was that black and Hispanic students who attended traditional public schools were at a disadvantage because the curriculum and culture didn't match their communities' culture or lifestyle in areas such as language, cultural traditions, or view of historic events leading to racism. Black House, with a black student body of 40 to 80 students and a black faculty, opened in 1970.[9] The school offered basic skills plus classes to raise black consciousness such as Black Nation Building and the Black Man and the Law. La Casa de la Raza opened as a Hispanic school in 1971. It was a bilingual school with a curriculum that was based on Chicano culture and values. Almost one-third of Berkeley's Chicano students attended La Casa. Both Black House and La Casa de la Raza were forced to close in 1973 for violating segregation laws under the Civil Rights Act. Today, ethnic studies classes, such as African American or Mexican American studies, are offered in some public schools to fill a gap in teaching students about US history and culture.

disproportionately on minority students, their opportunity for equal education was harmed. "Racially biased discipline is often the result of unacknowledged stereotypes of Latino and black students that result in their being suspended and expelled in disproportionately higher numbers than their white counterparts," said Eva Paterson, who is the president of the Equal Justice Society (EJS).[8] The EJS was one group that filed the 2014 suit.

In addition, it is often difficult for parents to transport their children to alternative schools. When Antonio M., whose full last name wasn't given, was accused of fighting, the Kern County school district assigned him to a community school 30 miles (48 km) from his home. His parents had no way to get him to school each day. When they tried to explain this to school officials, they were told that Antonio could travel by bus by making three transfers. If this didn't work, the officials suggested Antonio might ride a bicycle to school.

Reforms

In 2017, the Kern High School District in California reached an agreement with parents in the lawsuit that had charged the school with discrimination in its rates of suspension, expulsion, and transfers to alternative schools. The district agreed to create new policies regarding discipline. It would make these policies by consulting with experts on racial bias.

The California legislature also stepped in, prohibiting suspension of K–3 students for "willful defiance," including "talking back, dress code violations and failing to do homework or failing to have school supplies."[10] They also prohibited jailing students for truancy, although parents may be jailed for not attempting to keep students in school.

A NATIONAL PROBLEM

Kern County isn't the only school district where disciplinary practices have led to minority students being provided fewer educational opportunities than their white counterparts. The practice is seen in school districts across the country, where minority students are forced into less desirable schools or independent study, decreasing their chance to succeed in school.

According to the Civil Rights Project at the University of

School officials might unknowingly use bias against minorities when handing out punishments.

California, Los Angeles, out-of-school suspensions and expulsions rose steadily in the United States in the decades after 1970. These punishments were given out routinely for nonviolent as well as violent offenses. The trend has fallen most heavily on minority students. The years between 1973 and 2006 found that suspensions for black students rose from 6 to 15 percent across the country. The rate for Latinos grew from 3 to almost 7 percent, while for white students the rate grew from 3 percent to less than 5 percent.[11]

A study sponsored by the Council of State Governments, an organization with a mission to improve state policies by sharing information and ideas between states, tracked Texas students from seventh to twelfth grade. The 2011 report discovered that 60 percent of students had been expelled or suspended. In 97 percent of cases, discipline was given out by school officials rather than laws enforcing expulsion. After controlling for variables other than race, researchers found that black students were 31 percent more likely to get discretionary discipline than members of other racial groups.[12]

In 2011, the Obama administration announced that the Department of Education and Department of Justice would work together in a two-year effort to address issues related to aggressive discipline in the country's schools. Their joint committee, the Supportive School Discipline Initiative (SSDI), investigated complaints including the excessive suspensions of black children compared to white children accused of the same offense. In one study, the National Policy

Supportive School Discipline Initiative

The Supportive School Discipline Initiative created four pillars for addressing the issue of harsh school discipline. The first brings together research specialists, psychologists, legislators, educators, juvenile justice officials, local law enforcement, school officials, parents, and students to create policy and recommendations for change. The second pillar pays for data collection and analysis of discipline as it affects boys and girls and different ethnic and socioeconomic groups. The third pillar provides legal guidelines for schools regarding whether or not their disciplinary actions are in line with the Civil Rights Act of 1964. Finally, the fourth pillar supports new efforts to improve policy and practice related to school discipline.

Education Center found that in North Carolina in 2010, 32 percent of black students were suspended for first-time violations for using a cell phone, compared to 15 percent of white students with the same offense. For the first-time offense of public display of affection, 43 percent of black students were suspended, compared with 15 percent of white students with the same offense.[13]

DISCUSSION STARTERS

- Why do you think minority students are targeted more for school discipline than white students?

- Do you think teacher training might help reduce unfair punishment for minority students? Explain your answer.

- Do you think the government is doing enough to protect minority students' educational opportunities? Explain your reasoning.

CHAPTER EIGHT

MOVING BACKWARD

Toch oday's schools are more segregated than they were during the 1970s. The increasing racial segregation in schools is a result of several factors. Laws have changed how districts can integrate schools. The country's demographics have changed, with a smaller percentage of white students and a larger percentage of Hispanic and Asian students. Plus, research has shown that new factors, such as socioeconomic status, are an important component of racial segregation. Student transfers, unless they are designed to encourage integration, often increase segregation. This happens because families with a higher socioeconomic status can afford to transfer out of lower-income districts, while families with a lower socioeconomic status can't afford to go the other direction.

In the 2010s, some people still opposed racial integration.

From 1991 to 2009, the government allowed hundreds of school districts to shake off desegregation court orders. A 2011 study in the *Journal of Policy Analysis and Management* found that racial segregation increased in schools after their release from desegregation orders, compared with schools that remained under orders. It wasn't clear to the study's authors why many of the schools were released, as they were similar to other districts that weren't released. The rate of increase in segregation was gradual over many years and occurred most often in elementary schools, in big school districts, and in areas with a large black population. At the height of efforts to integrate the country, 750 school districts across the United States were under desegregation orders.[1] By 2014, more than 300 school districts remained under desegregation orders.[2] But many courts are releasing schools from desegregation orders because courts haven't followed up on the orders over the decades and the judges have no idea what is happening in the school districts. For example, the lawyer for the Hollandale, Mississippi, school district didn't even know if the order to desegregate was still being enforced. In Washington, Georgia, the lawyer for the district thought the desegregation order, which is still in effect, had been lifted in 2000.

AFFIRMATIVE ACTION UNDER FIRE

In 1965, President Lyndon B. Johnson issued an executive order requiring all federal contractors, including university campuses, to create affirmative action plans or risk losing federal money. Universities developed plans to actively promote admission, hiring, and promotion of minorities and women within their systems. Universities were also required to provide information about affirmative action policies and enforce the rules.

By the 1970s, however, affirmative action was weakened, especially in universities. In 1978, the Supreme Court ruled in *Regents of the University of California v. Bakke* that race could be one factor in selecting among qualified students for admission. However, it also ruled that the university medical school's policy of reserving 16 seats out of 100 for disadvantaged minority students in each entering class was unconstitutional.[3] So, although race could be considered as one component in a student's application, a policy of rationing seats by race wasn't allowed.

In 1995, the Board of Regents of the University of California adopted resolutions overturning the system's affirmative action policies. As of 1996, the university no longer considered race or gender in its hiring practices. As of 1997 for graduate programs and 1998

Regents of University of California v. Bakke

Alan Bakke, a white man, applied to the medical school at the University of California, Davis two years in a row and was turned down both times. The university only had 100 seats open each year in the school, and 16 of those seats were reserved for disadvantaged or racial minority students.[4] Bakke's grades were better than any of the students who got the reserved seats, so he sued the university for discriminating against him due to his race. The case went to the California Supreme Court. It ruled that Bakke must be admitted, and that the admission system violated the Equal Protection Clause of the Fourteenth Amendment. The US Supreme Court reviewed the case, ruling that race couldn't be the only factor in deciding admissions but could be one factor among others.

for undergraduate programs, it no longer considered race in its admissions policy. In addition, California voters in 1996 chose to amend their state constitution, stating, in part, that the state couldn't discriminate against or grant preferential treatment to any race in public education. The case was appealed to the US Supreme Court, which let the lower court's ruling stand.

Proponents of affirmative action pushed to repeal the law. They argued that the end of affirmative action had resulted in a drop in black and Hispanic first-year students at the university. They also pointed out that minority students felt the university was less welcoming. In 1998, the University of California, Berkeley had a 61 percent drop in first-year admissions of African American, Hispanic, and Native American students.[5] At the University of California, Los Angeles minority admissions declined by 36 percent.[6] Still, the law stood.

Did Affirmative Action Work?

Affirmative action has given minorities some gains, but it has not achieved equality at the top colleges. According to a 2017 *New York Times* analysis, Hispanic and black students "are more underrepresented at top colleges than 35 years ago." Black students make up 22 percent of college-age Americans but are just 13 percent of college freshmen at top colleges. There is still a 9 percent gap between Hispanic freshmen at top colleges and the percent of the college-age population that is Hispanic.[7]

Some people think affirmative action helps female and minority students.

DEFEAT OF AFFIRMATIVE ACTION

In the early 2000s, affirmative action was frequently challenged in court, and cases from many states dealing with university admissions were heard. In general, US District Courts upheld that race could be considered as one part of an overall decision for college admission. In the 2003 case *Grutter v. Bollinger*, the Supreme Court agreed that race could be a factor in admissions at the University of Michigan because of "an educational benefit that flows from student diversity."[8] The ruling meant diversity through affirmative action was still allowed, although it couldn't take priority over other qualifications.

The use of affirmative action for K–12 schools, especially actions such as busing that caused upheavals in communities, also came under fire. In 1999, a US district court ended the mandatory integration of schools in Charlotte, North Carolina. In *Capacchione v. Charlotte-Mecklenburg Schools*, the court determined that the schools had made a good faith effort to integrate, so there was no longer any reason for them to remain under a federal desegregation order. Busing stopped and students returned to their neighborhood schools. However, segregation increased, as the neighborhoods were divided into rich and poor communities. Shortly after, other communities began to be released from desegregation orders.

Finally, in 2007, the Supreme Court made a decision in *Parents Involved in Community Schools v. Seattle School District No. 1* that was the death blow to affirmative action in K–12 schools. The case involved two school districts, the Seattle County School District and the Jefferson County School District. Seattle let students pick their high school. However, when a lot of students picked a single school, selection was based on siblings at the school and race. Jefferson had a rule that no more than 50 percent of students at a particular school could be black.[9] Some parents whose children were rejected from transfers based on race filed a lawsuit.

The court ruled that the districts didn't fall under the ruling in *Grutter* where race was one factor to achieving a diverse

Abigail Fisher spoke to reporters while her case was being reviewed by the Supreme Court.

student body in higher education. Rather, as race was the only determining factor for entry for many students, the court ruled in favor of the plaintiffs. It was a defeat for affirmative action in K–12 schools.

DISCRIMINATION FROM AFFIRMATIVE ACTION?

Abigail Fisher is white and lived in Texas. She was rejected from the University of Texas at Austin for the 2008 school year. She brought a suit against the school, stating that the rejection hurt her equal protection rights under the Fourteenth Amendment. Fisher said she was denied when minority students with credentials not as good as hers were accepted. In *Fisher v. University of Texas*, the Supreme Court ruled that universities could use race as one factor in determining admissions. However, it went beyond *Grutter* in saying that race could only be used as a factor if the university had already tried in good faith other measures to achieve diversity. Because the University of Texas met the standard for a limited use of race for admissions, Fisher lost the case.

However, the use of race as a component for college admission, especially for the most elite universities in the United States, continues to be under fire. Writer P. R. Lockhart notes, "Data shows that Asian-American students are overrepresented at many of America's most selective schools. At Harvard for example, Asian American students were roughly 22 percent of those admitted in 2017 but Asian Americans were just 5 percent of the population."[10] In addition, even with affirmative action, black and Hispanic students have less representation at the top universities than they had 35 years ago.

Redrawing District Lines

In 2013, Memphis, Tennessee, tried to reduce racial segregation in its urban schools by redrawing district lines. The newly drawn district merged primarily black Memphis schools with some of the surrounding county schools that had more white students. The next year, six surrounding cities seceded from the new district, making five of the new districts more predominantly white than the original district had been.

NEW DISTRICTS

In addition to ending forced desegregation in many cases,

recent court decisions have allowed suburbs to split off into new school districts instead of being part of larger districts that may include urban schools. Since 2000, 71 areas in the United States have seceded from their school districts.[11] These new districts tend to be much whiter than the old districts.

One example of such a split is a wealthy community in the San Francisco Bay area. Northgate High School and the nearby elementary and middle schools are part of the Mount Diablo School District. In 2017, the area containing Northgate, with a median household income of $126,000, proposed breaking away from Mount Diablo, where the median household income is about $76,000.[12] The school board didn't approve the plan because it felt the split would create unequal school districts. Mount Diablo is about 31 percent white and 42 percent Hispanic.[13] The proposed Northgate District was estimated to become 65 percent white and 8 percent Hispanic.[14]

DISCUSSION STARTERS

- Do you think affirmative action is fair? Explain your reasoning.

- Does the government have a responsibility to enforce desegregation throughout the nation? Explain your answer.

- Do you think it's fair that suburbs can form their own school districts? Explain your opinion.

CHAPTER NINE

SOLUTIONS

Since the 2007 Supreme Court ruling *Parents Involved in Community Schools v. Seattle School District No. 1*, which virtually barred schools from using race as a factor in assigning students to schools, there has been a move to make educational opportunities more equal by using socioeconomic factors to desegregate schools. Research has shown that the difference in income between districts in a state, or even within a school district, has increased since 1990. In the biggest 100 school districts in the United States, economic segregation increased around 30 percent between 1991 and 2010.[1] According to the US Department of Education, wealthy districts spend 15.6 percent more per student than low-income districts.[2] Since black students are four times as likely to be in a poor school, desegregation by income often equals racial desegregation.[3]

Some schools are forced to close down because of a lack of funding.

 The Connecticut Supreme Court ruled in the case *Connecticut Coalition for Justice in Education Funding (CCJEF) v. Rell.*

Connecticut is one of the country's wealthiest states, yet many of its students attend poor schools. In the state's wealthy districts, students have access to guidance counselors and personal laptops. In poorer districts where students need more help, teachers are paid less, and there are fewer counselors and tutors. According to the State Department of Education, the wealthiest districts, such as Greenwich, spend $6,000 more per pupil a year than a poor district such as Bridgeport.[4] Greenwich is almost 80 percent white.[5] Bridgeport is more than 71 percent black and Hispanic.[6]

In 2005, a group of citizens sued the state for the inequality in *Connecticut Coalition for Justice in Education Funding (CCJEF) v. Rell.* An earlier lawsuit filed in 1977 had required the state to redistribute some funding, but the new lawsuit claimed that hasn't been adequately done. Although the lower court decided in favor of CCJEF, the Connecticut Supreme Court overturned the decision, finding that adequate funding, as defined by the state constitution, was being provided to all schools.

WHAT STATES ARE DOING

Many states are struggling to fund schools. Schools that are in low socioeconomic areas have been hit hardest, especially in finding quality classroom teachers. However, teacher pay is low in many areas, so it's difficult to recruit the best teachers.

Keeping good teachers, especially in low-income schools, should be a high priority because research has shown the importance of good teachers. The Learning Policy Institute, an

What States Spend

Average spending on schools per state in the 2014–2015 school year was $11,454 per pupil. New York spent the most money per pupil at $20,744. This was more than three times what the lowest-spending state, Utah, spent at $6,751 per pupil.[7] The other highest-spending states were Alaska, Connecticut, New Jersey, Vermont, Massachusetts, and Wyoming. The District of Columbia was also a high-spending area. Massachusetts, New Jersey, Vermont, Connecticut, Wyoming, and New York were ranked among the top ten states for overall school quality by Education Week, a news organization that covers K–12 education. In Alaska, which didn't make the top-ten list for quality schools, funding is variable because it depends on oil revenues. Washington, DC, although not in the top-ten list for quality, ranks among the fastest-improving schools in the country. Along with Utah, the states of Nevada, Mississippi, Idaho, Oklahoma, Alabama, Arizona, and Texas all ranked at the bottom for school spending. They also all ranked below fortieth in school quality.

Keeping good teachers in minority schools can help students succeed academically.

organization that conducts research to improve education, has listed criteria for achieving this goal. They include economic incentives such as higher pay, forgiveness of student loans, or other workplace incentives such as childcare and housing subsidies. Even with low pay, many teachers leave the profession due to work conditions. Strengthening support for teachers from administrators and principals can often encourage teachers to stay. In addition, laws that govern the movement of teachers from state to state should allow teachers to more easily go to places where they are needed.

LOCAL EFFORTS

Since the 2007 ruling that undermined racial desegregation in K–12 schools, some school districts have adopted plans that integrate schools based on socioeconomic status rather than race.

The most common method to achieve socioeconomic equality between schools is to redraw school district boundaries. However, this doesn't work in school districts where almost all of the students are minorities, which is the case in many urban school districts. In these situations, it may be necessary to integrate across district lines. Although magnet and charter schools have at times succeeded at desegregation, their placement can also lead to more segregated schools.

Controlled choice options allow parents and students the chance to choose the school they want. These plans have been successful when they are carefully crafted to increase diversity while at the same time take into account the hardships parents and students face, such as transportation or siblings attending different schools.

Still, progress has been slow. As of 2016, of the 15,000 school districts in the United States, only about 100 use socioeconomic

A Grassroots Effort

Another effort toward desegregation has been to encourage white parents who believe in integrating schools to enroll their own children in minority schools. Integrated Schools, founded by Courtney Everts Mykytyn of Los Angeles in 2014, uses school visits and promotional events and literature to provide parents and students with information about making the decision to integrate.

factors to desegregate. That means that of the 50 million students in K–12 schools, 92 percent them are in schools with people from similar racial and socioeconomic backgrounds.[8]

Free Lunch

Student eligibility to receive federally funded free or reduced cost lunch has long been used as an indicator of student income. However, this indicator has become less reliable with time. The family income is self-reported on application forms for free lunch and may be inaccurate. High school students often don't apply for free lunch due to the stigma of having a low income. In 2010, Congress passed legislation that allowed entire districts to become eligible for free lunch. In these districts, it's impossible to tell exactly how many students are actually eligible for free or reduced lunch. These factors make it difficult to determine the socioeconomic makeup of the student body.

SCHOOL DIVERSITY

School diversity, both racial and socioeconomic, has been a major struggle in the United States. Early in the country's history, equal education opportunities were denied to Native Americans, African Americans, and other ethnic groups. *Plessy v. Ferguson* demonstrated that separate schools were not equal schools. *Brown v. Board of Education* officially ended segregation, but it took further legal action to force school districts to begin desegregation. But over time, courts eased the regulatory oversight, and segregation has slowly returned. Today, integrating schools is often a local effort from parents

and school officials who believe that integrated schools are better schools.

School diversity produces better classrooms for learning for all students. Diverse classrooms reduce racial bias while improving complex reasoning and creativity. School diversity is a goal that parents, students, and governments should continue to fight for, but the end goal should be true integration. This would let all students participate equally to achieve a quality education.

DISCUSSION STARTERS

- What can states do to encourage people to become teachers?

- Do you think that racial integration is necessary for equal educational opportunities for all?

- Do you think socioeconomic integration will achieve racial integration?

ESSENTIAL FACTS

SIGNIFICANT EVENTS

- In 1896, the Supreme Court ruled in *Plessy v. Ferguson* that separate but equal facilities were allowed in the United States. This ruling supported segregation of the races in many areas of life, including housing, transportation, and schools.

- In 1950, the Supreme Court decided in the case *Sweatt v. Painter* that the School of Law of the State University for Negroes was inferior to the University of Texas Law School. The court declared that Heman Marion Sweatt must be allowed into the University of Texas Law School. The ruling ended segregation at the school.

- *Brown v. Board of Education* was a landmark Supreme Court case in 1954 that ended legal segregation in education and overturned *Plessy v. Ferguson*.

- The Civil Rights Act of 1964, in part, allowed the US Justice Department to file lawsuits against segregated school districts.

- The 2007 court case *Parents Involved in Community Schools v. Seattle School District No. 1* dealt a hard defeat for affirmative action.

KEY PLAYERS

- The NAACP formed in the early 1900s and fought for equal rights for people of color. The organization was involved in many court cases that centered on equal educational opportunities for African Americans.

- Thurgood Marshall was an attorney who helped bring about desegregation in education. He was also the first African American justice on the US Supreme Court.

- In 1957, the Little Rock Nine enrolled in an all-white high school in Arkansas, testing desegregation efforts. The white backlash against the students was fierce, and President Dwight D. Eisenhower sent US troops to protect the students as they attended school.

IMPACT ON SOCIETY

Laws affect students' educational opportunities. In the first half of the 1900s, laws concerning school segregation reinforced the notion that races were not equal. Since *Brown v. Board of Education* in 1954, laws tried to bring change in society by requiring desegregation in schools. Integrated schools are known to have positive benefits for students, yet there are many segregated school districts across the United States today.

QUOTE

"Segregation of white and colored children in public schools has a detrimental effect upon the colored children. The impact is greater when it has the sanction of the law, for the policy of separating the races is usually interpreted as denoting the inferiority of the Negro group. . . . We conclude that . . . the doctrine of 'separate but equal' has no place. Separate educational facilities are inherently unequal."

—*Chief Justice Earl Warren in the 1954* Brown v. Board of Education *decision*

GLOSSARY

appeal
A request for a higher court to review the decision of a lower court.

brief
A written document of an argument providing points and evidence as to why the side writing the brief should win the case.

civil rights
A guarantee of equal social opportunities and equal protection under the law, regardless of gender, race, religion, or other personal traits.

deliberation
A long and careful consideration of a matter, especially by a judge.

demographics
Statistical data relating to the population as a whole, or to particular groups within it, showing factors such as race, age, income, or education.

integrate
To make schools, parks, and other facilities available to people of all races on an equal basis.

lawsuit
A dispute that is taken to a court of law.

mandatory
Required.

opinion
A statement by a court on the legality of an issue.

plaintiff
The one accusing a defendant in a court of law.

precedent
In court cases, a ruling on a case that serves as a guide for future related rulings.

segregation
The practice of separating groups of people based on race, gender, ethnicity, or other factors.

violate
To break a rule.

ADDITIONAL RESOURCES

SELECTED BIBLIOGRAPHY

Bowman, Kristi L. (ed). *The Pursuit of Racial and Ethnic Equality in American Public Schools*. Michigan State UP, 2015.

Minow, Martha. *In Brown's Wake: Legacies of America's Educational Landmark*. Oxford UP, 2010.

Ryan, James E. *Five Miles Away, A World Apart: One City, Two Schools, and the Story of Educational Opportunity in Modern America*. Oxford UP, 2010.

FURTHER READINGS

Harris, Duchess, and Laura K. Murray. *Class and Race*. Abdo, 2019.

Harris, Duchess, and Gail Radley. *The Impact of Slavery in America*. Abdo, 2020.

ONLINE RESOURCES

To learn more about education, race, and the law, please visit **abdobooklinks.com** or scan this QR code. These links are routinely monitored and updated to provide the most current information available.

MORE INFORMATION

For more information on this subject, contact or visit the following organizations:

BROWN V. BOARD OF EDUCATION NATIONAL HISTORIC SITE

1515 SE Monroe St.

Topeka, Kansas 66612-1143

785-354-4273

nps.gov/brvb

This national historic site offers exhibits focusing on racism in education, the civil rights movement, and more.

NATIONAL MUSEUM OF AFRICAN AMERICAN HISTORY AND CULTURE

1400 Constitution Ave. NW

Washington, DC 20560

844-750-3012

nmaahc.si.edu

The National Museum of African American History & Culture opened in 2016. This museum has tens of thousands of artifacts illuminating African American history and culture. There are also exhibits on the history of slavery.

SOURCE NOTES

CHAPTER 1. LACKING OPPORTUNITIES

1. "To See Divide between Rich Schools and Poor, Look to Waukegan and Stevenson." *Chicago Tribune*, 6 Sept. 2016, chicagotribune.com. Accessed 26 June 2019.

2. "To See Divide between Rich Schools and Poor, Look to Waukegan and Stevenson."

3. Valeria Strauss. "The Real Story of New Orleans and Its Charter Schools." *Washington Post*, 4 Sept. 2018, washingtonpost.com. Accessed 26 June 2019.

4. "To See Divide between Rich Schools and Poor, Look to Waukegan and Stevenson."

5. Linda Darling-Hammond. "Unequal Opportunity: Race and Education." *Brookings*, 1 Mar. 1998, brookings.edu. Accessed 26 June 2019.

6. "Unequal Opportunity: Race and Education."

7. "Unequal Opportunity: Race and Education."

8. Alexander Nazaryan. "School Segregation in America Is as Bad Today as It Was in the 1960s." *Newsweek*, 22 Mar. 2018, newsweek.com. Accessed 26 June 2019.

9. "Unequal Opportunity: Race and Education."

10. Richard D. Kahlenberg. "School Integration's Comeback." *Atlantic*, 10 Feb. 2016, theatlantic.com. Accessed 26 June 2019.

11. "School Segregation in America Is as Bad Today as It Was in the 1960s."

CHAPTER 2. LEGAL SEGREGATION

1. David Carleton. "Old Deluder Satan Act of 1647." *Middle Tennessee State University*, n.d., mtsu.edu. Accessed 26 June 2019.

2. "Brown v. Board at Fifty: 'With an Even Hand.'" *Library of Congress*, n.d., loc.gov. Accessed 26 June 2019.

3. "The Case of Mrs. Margaret Douglass." *PBS*, n.d., pbs.org. Accessed 26 June 2019.

4. "Education, Arts, & Culture." *Thirteen*, n.d., thirteen.org. Accessed 26 June 2019.

5. "J. W. Cumming, James S. Harper, and John C. Ladeveze v. County Board of Education of Richmond County, State of Georgia." *Cornell Law School*, n.d., law.cornell.edu. Accessed 26 June 2019.

6. "Brown v. Board at Fifty: 'With An Even Hand.'"

7. "NAACP." *History*, 13 Mar. 2019, history.com. Accessed 26 June 2019.

8. "Brown v. Board at Fifty: 'With an Even Hand.'"

9. "Loleta Union School District's Violations of Title VI of the Civil Rights Act of 1964." *Youth Law*, 18 Dec. 2013, youthlaw.org. Accessed 26 June 2019.

10. Allen Woods. "A Hidden Tribe, a Disastrous School and Finally, a Cry for Help." *AZ Central*, 20 Apr. 2017, azcentral.com. Accessed 26 June 2019.

11. Susan Brenna. "The U.S. Once Used Schools to Try to Exterminate Native Language and Culture. A New Approach Would Build on Indigenous Values, Languages, and Strengths." *Teach for America*, 11 Dec. 2014, teachforamerica.org. Accessed 26 June 2019.

12. "Public High School Graduation Rates." *National Center for Education Statistics*, May 2019, nces.ed.gov. Accessed 26 June 2019.

CHAPTER 3. BREAKTHROUGHS IN HIGHER EDUCATION

1. "Thurgood Marshall." *History*, 7 June 2019, history.com. Accessed 26 June 2019.
2. "The First GI Bill and the Disparity for Black Veterans." *Fight4Vets*, n.d., fight4vets.com. Accessed 26 June 2019.

CHAPTER 4. *BROWN V. BOARD OF EDUCATION*

1. "Mendez v. Westminster School District of Orange County." *Civics Resources*, n.d., texasbar.com. Accessed 26 June 2019.
2. "Kenneth and Mamie Clark Doll." *NPS*, 10 Apr. 2015, nps.gov. Accessed 26 June 2019.
3. "Brown v. Board of Education." *Cornell Law School*, n.d., law.cornell.edu. Accessed 26 June 2019.
4. "Brown v. Board of Education." *NPS*, 10 Apr. 2015, nps.gov. Accessed 26 June 2019.
5. "Bolling v. Sharpe." *NPS*, 10 July 2017, nps.gov. Accessed 26 June 2019.
6. "Davis v. County School Board." *NPS*, 10 Apr. 2015, nps.gov. Accessed 26 June 2019.

CHAPTER 5. INTEGRATION BEGINS

1. "School Desegregation." *Legal Dictionary*, n.d., legal-dictionary.thefreedictionary.com. Accessed 26 June 2019.
2. "Little Rock Central High School Desegregation Silver Dollar." *United States Mint*, 1 June 2016, usmint.gov. Accessed 26 June 2019.
3. "School Desegregation."
4. "Why Is This Happening?" *NBC News*, 31 July 2018, nbcnews.com. Accessed 26 June 2019.
5. "Green v. County School Board of New Kent County." *Cornell Law School*, n.d., law.cornell.edu. Accessed 26 June 2019.
6. "Swann v. Charlotte-Mecklenburg Board of Education." *Cornell Law School*, n.d., law.cornell.edu. Accessed 26 June 2019.

CHAPTER 6. CHOICE

1. Hayley Glatter. "The School-Voucher Paradox." *Atlantic*, 15 Feb. 2017, theatlantic.com. Accessed 26 June 2019.
2. "Charter Schools." *National Center for Education Statistics*, n.d., nces.ed.gov. Accessed 26 June 2019.
3. "Report: Voucher, Charter Schools Consume $193m in State Aid." *US News*, 28 Mar. 2019, usnews.com. Accessed 26 June 2019.
4. "KIPP." *KIPP*, n.d., kipp.org. Accessed 26 June 2019.
5. Richard Whitmire. "Top Charter Networks Becoming District-Size." *HuffPost*, 21 Oct. 2014, huffpost.com. Accessed 26 June 2019.
6. "Top Charter Networks Becoming District-Size."

CHAPTER 7. DISCIPLINE IN SCHOOLS

1. Susan Ferriss. "An Epidemic of Expulsions." *Center for Public Integrity*, 14 Oct. 2014, publicintegrity.org. Accessed 26 June 2019.

2. Susan Ferriss. "Suit against Kern County Schools Alleges Disproportionate Discipline for Minorities." *Center for Public Integrity*, 17 Oct. 2014, publicintegrity.org. Accessed 26 June 2019.

3. "An Epidemic of Expulsions."

4. "Suit against Kern County Schools Alleges Disproportionate Discipline for Minorities."

5. "Suit against Kern County Schools Alleges Disproportionate Discipline for Minorities."

6. "An Epidemic of Expulsions."

7. "An Epidemic of Expulsions."

8. Jane Meredith Adams. "Settlement in Kern Discrimination Lawsuit Calls for New School Discipline Policies." *EdSource*, 24 July 2017, edsource.org. Accessed 26 June 2019.

9. "Black House." *Berkeley Revolution*, n.d., revolution.berkeley.edu. Accessed 26 June 2019.

10. Susan Ferriss. "California Takes on Harsh Discipline and Academic Inequities for Black, Latino Students." *Center for Public Integrity*, 29 Oct. 2014, publicintegrity.org. Accessed 26 June 2019.

11. "An Epidemic of Expulsions."

12. "An Epidemic of Expulsions."

13. Susan Ferriss. "New Report Cites Disproportionate Punishment for Black Students." *Center for Public Integrity*, 19 May 2014, publicintegrity.org. Accessed 26 June 2019.

CHAPTER 8. MOVING BACKWARD

1. Nikole Hannah-Jones. "School District Still Faces Fights—and Confusion—on Integration." *Atlantic*, 2 May 2014, theatlantic.com. Accessed 26 June 2019.

2. "School District Still Faces Fights—and Confusion—on Integration."

3. "Regents of the Univ. of Cal. v. Bakke." *Cornell Law School*, n.d., law.cornell.edu. Accessed 26 June 2019.

4. "Regents of the Univ. of Cal. v. Bakke."

5. "More History of Affirmative Action Policies from the 1960s." *American Association for Access, Equity and Diversity*, n.d., aaaed.org. Accessed 26 June 2019.

6. "More History of Affirmative Action Policies from the 1960s."

7. Jeremy Ashkenas, Haeyoun Park, and Adam Pearce. "Even with Affirmative Action, Blacks and Hispanics Are More Underrepresented at Top Colleges Than 35 Years Ago." *New York Times*, 24 Aug. 2017, nytimes.com. Accessed 26 June 2019.

8. "More History of Affirmative Action Policies from the 1960s."

9. "Parents Involved in Community Schools v. Seattle School District." *Case Briefs*, n.d., casebriefs.com. Accessed 26 June 2019.

10. P. R. Lockhart. "The Lawsuit against Harvard That Could Change Affirmative Action in College Admissions, Explained." *Vox*, 18 Oct. 2018, vox.com. Accessed 26 June 2019.

11. Laura Bliss. "School Secession Is Segregation." *City Lab*, 26 June 2017, citylab.com. Accessed 26 June 2019.

12. Alexander Nazaryan. "Whites Only: School Segregation Is Back, from Birmingham to San Francisco." *Newsweek*, 2 May 2017, newsweek.com. Accessed 26 June 2019.

13. "Fast Facts about the Mt. Diablo Unified School District." *Mt. Diablo Unified School District*, n.d., mdusd-ca.schoolloop.com. Accessed 26 June 2019.

14. "Whites Only: School Segregation Is Back, From Birmingham to San Francisco."

CHAPTER 9. SOLUTIONS

1. Halley Potter and Kimberly Quick. "The Secret to School Integration." *New York Times*, 23 Feb. 2016, nytimes.com. Accessed 27 June 2019.

2. Alana Semuels. "Good School, Rich School; Bad School, Poor School." *Atlantic*, 25 Aug. 2016, theatlantic.com. Accessed 27 June 2019.

3. Grover J. "Russ" Whitehurst, Richard V. Reeves, Edward Rodrigue. "Segregation, Race, and Charter Schools: What Do We Know?" *Brookings*, 24 Oct. 2016, brookings.edu. Accessed 27 June 2019.

4. "Good School, Rich School; Bad School, Poor School."

5. "Greenwich, Connecticut." *City-Data*, n.d., city-data.com. Accessed 27 June 2019.

6. "Bridgeport, Connecticut." *City-Data*, n.d., city-data.com. Accessed 27 June 2019.

7. Kevin Mahnken. "The States That Spend the Most (and Least) on Education—and How Their Students Perform Compared with Their Neighbors." *74 Million*, 9 Jan. 2018, the74million.org. Accessed 27 June 2019.

8. Melinda D. Anderson. "The Promise of Integrated Schools." *Atlantic*, 16 Feb. 2016, theatlantic.com. Accessed 27 June 2019.

INDEX

ABOUT THE AUTHORS

DUCHESS HARRIS, JD, PHD

Dr. Harris is a professor of American Studies at Macalester College and curator of the Duchess Harris Collection of ABDO books. She is also the coauthor of the titles in the collection, which features popular selections such as *Hidden Human Computers: The Black Women of NASA* and series including News Literacy and Being Female in America.

Before working with ABDO, Dr. Harris authored several other books on the topics of race, culture, and American history. She served as an associate editor for *Litigation News*, the American Bar Association Section of Litigation's quarterly flagship publication, and was the first editor in chief of *Law Raza*, an interactive online journal covering race and the law, published at William Mitchell College of Law. She has earned a PhD in American Studies from the University of Minnesota and a JD from William Mitchell College of Law.

CYNTHIA KENNEDY HENZEL

Cynthia Kennedy Henzel has a BS in social studies education and an MS in geography. She has worked as a teacher-educator in many countries. Currently, she writes books and develops education materials for social studies, history, science, and ELL students. She has written more than 85 books for young people.